ADDICTED TO
FISHING.

MW00737791

George Peters

A PLUME BOOK

PLUME
Published by the Penguin Group
Penguin Books USA Inc., 375 Hudson Street,
New York, New York 10014, U.S.A.
Penguin Books Ltd, 27 Wrights Lane,
London W8 5TZ, England
Penguin Books Australia Ltd, Ringwood,
Victoria, Australia
Penguin Books Canada Ltd, 2801 John Street,
Markham, Ontario, Canada L3R 1B4
Penguin Books (N.Z.) Ltd, 182-190 Wairau Road,
Auckland 10, New Zealand

Penguin Books Ltd, Registered Offices:
Harmondsworth, Middlesex, England

First published by Plume, an imprint of New American Library,
a division of Penguin Books USA Inc.

First Printing, May 1991
10 9 8 7 6 5 4 3 2 1

LIBRARY OF CONGRESS CATALOGING-IN-PUBLICATION DATA

Peters, George.
    Addicted to fishing! / George Peters.
        p.   cm.
    ISBN 0-452-26613-0
    1. Fishing—Humor.   2. Fishing—Caricatures and cartoons.
3. American wit and humor, Pictorial.   I. Title.
PN6231.F5P38   1991
741.5'973—dc20   90-24221
                                                    CIP

Printed in the United States of America
Set in ITC Quorum Book

The Official Fishing-Addiction Test

For some people fishing is just a relaxing pastime; for others it can be a way of life—a consuming passion. Here are a few quick questions to help determine if you, too, are *Addicted to Fishing*:

Yes or **No**

——— Do you laugh and cry during TV fishing programs?
——— Do you ever talk to your bait?
——— Does it ever talk back?
——— Has your significant other ever complained about bait in the fridge?
——— Have you ever used your wife's earrings as spinner blade components?

If you answered yes to any of the above questions, cheer up, you're not alone. Keep a tight line and proceed to the next page—for laughs, for fun, because this is the book for everyone who is . . .

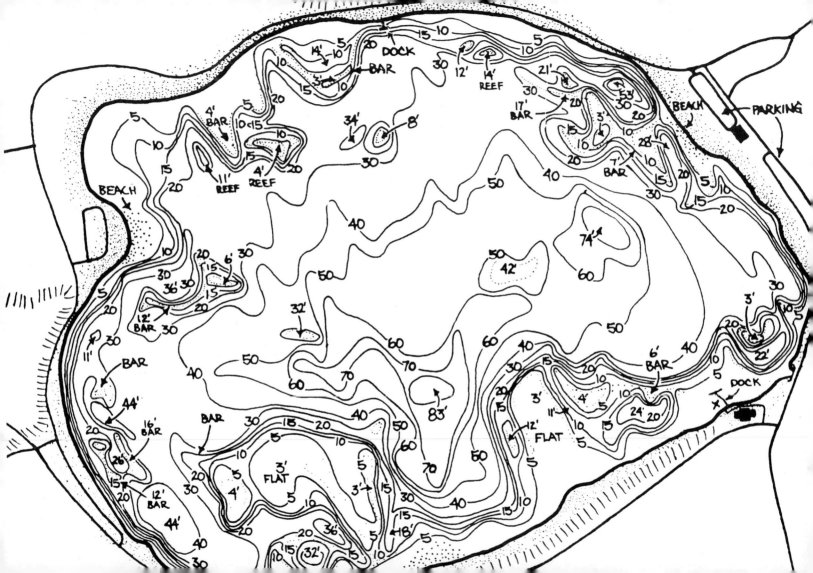

ACKNOWLEDGMENTS

Life is hard. Then you die. Fortunately, for some of us, there is fishing in between. And for a few of us, there is a book about fishing in between that.

I would like to gratefully acknowledge the following people who helped—each in his own way—to make this book possible.

First, there is my dad, who started it all many, many fishing seasons ago by taking me perch fishing along the banks of the Niagara River. I would also like to thank my mom, who packed the sandwiches and gave me endless encouragement then, just as she does today. Also my brother Mike who, thank heavens, didn't drown at the foot of Ferry Street when the Giant Sheephead from Hell that was bigger than he was pulled him in. And my sister Kathy, who screamed like crazy every time Mike and I chased her around the house with dripping perch heads.

And of course, I would like to thank my loving wife Katherine, who put up with all the anxieties that go along with an author and his book.

My good buddy Paul Jacobs, who introduced me to my favorite obsession: smallies and brown trout. Break out the Jumbo Hose for Design Guys Kern Olson and Mav Engelhart—purveyors of good taste and bad jokes. A loud "Thanks, guys!" to writers Steve Schwartz, Tim Harkness, and Frank Schmidt for the editing, proofreading, and dumb suggestions that I never used. "Yo, dude!" to Doug Stange at *In-Fisherman Magazine* for publishing my first cartoon. And double high-fives to "G-Man," Glenn Meyer at *Outdoor News* for publishing the most cartoons. A major Design Guy Award to Chuck Nelson of Nelson Graphic Design for having a great sense of humor. And *extremely large* thanks to Rosemary Ahern at Plume Books for introducing me to Editor Heaven. And lastly, head butts and high-fives to my agent, Jeanne Hanson, for breaking a few records and being the best literary agent a cartoonist could ever hope to work with.

I would like to thank the following people and publications for publishing my cartoons:

Gary Ball . . . . *Angler and Hunter*
Dave Csanda . . . . *Angling Adventures*
Tim Kjos . . . . *Detroit Lakes Tribune*
Rod Bond and John Randolph . . . . *Fly Fisherman*
Dick Norlander . . . . *Mille Lacs Messenger*
Sam Gross . . . . *National Lampoon*
Glenn Meyer . . . . *Outdoor News*
Doug Stange . . . . *The In-Fisherman*
Steven Pennaz . . . . . . *The North American Fisherman*

·CONTENTS·

The Futility Begins

The desire to fish has been part of human nature ever since that fateful moment, a zillion fishing seasons ago, when primitive man came upon his first ancient, lily-pad–infested bay. He slipped his crude dugout canoe through the shallows, where he spotted the earliest ancestor of the largemouth bass. He parted his prehistoric lips in amazement and grunted the barely discernible words: "Yo! Hawg Heaven!"

And so the chase began. And so the futility began. After all, catching fish from a dugout canoe with your bare hands is no day at the beach, especially if you have a Neanderthal IQ that is equal to a night crawler with brain damage. Then, one day, something happened. Something big. After trying for weeks to catch a particularly large fish by hand, an angry Neanderthal, having given up, threw his spear at the fish out of pure frustration.

He nailed that sucker right between the eyes. And so a new and vastly improved fishing technique was born, which changed our sport forever.

After a long time and a lot of evolution, some enterprising Barney Rubble kinda guy laid down his spear and tied a sharp, curved bone to a braided line and named it "a hook and line." This breakthrough concept totally revolutionized fishing, but it had one very major drawback—namely, getting a bone sharp enough to catch fish. Incredible as it may seem, we are *still* frustrated by that very same drawback. You can hear fishermen across the country voicing the very same complaint their prehistoric predecessors voiced millennia ago: *"If they can put a friggin' man on the friggin' moon, they oughta be able to make a hook that's sharp right outta the friggin' pack!"* Eventually, some clever rockhead stuck a worm on his hook and noticed it caught a heck of a lot more fish than a bare hook did. And so fishing entered the Modern Era of Angling, and incidentally, the first bait shop was born.

Fishing as a Reason for Living

There are basically two types of fishermen in this world: the Moderate Fishermen and the Obsessed Fishermen.

The Moderate Fishermen approach fishing as a relaxing pastime. They like to get away now and then for a few hours of leisure fishing. It's an interesting approach, but frankly, when it comes to fishing, moderation is a concept I have never been able to comprehend. In fact, moderate fishing is so unappealing

BEFORE   AFTER

The transformation from a Moderate Fisherman to an Obsessed Fisherman can be startling.

to me, I would rather develop a severe case of intestinal parasites than pursue my sport with anything less than sheer determination.

The Obsessed Fishermen, on the other hand, approach their sport with an intensity that would make a pit bull on crack seem timid by comparison. For them, fishing is not a hobby. Fishing is a way of life, a reason for living. They are the chosen few. The obsessed, the select millions who like fishing in all its various forms using the word "like" as in "I like to breathe."

Why would we rather fish than do anything else? Because basically, the alternatives stink. Let's face it: When Saturday rolls around, you're stuck with four basic options:

OPTION 1: *More Work.* Choose this option and you get to go down to the office and put in an extra day of anxiety at the stress factory. This option

includes boot licking and idea crushing. You do the boot licking, and you guessed it—your ideas get crushed. *Helpful Tips:* Keep your eyes lowered and never, ever speak up.

OPTION 2: *Wife Duty.* How about spending a cozy weekend with your significant other? Just the two of you alone to spend uninterrupted quality time rekindling the old flame o'love. *Caution:* Be sure to check the calendar first. Otherwise, you might pick the wrong weekend of the month and wind up with PMS EVIL TWIN FROM HELL. A frightening thought, but sometimes unavoidable during the monsoon season. *Helpful Tips:* Remove belt and shoelaces before entering a weekend of Wife Duty.

OPTION 3: *Yard Work.* Manual Labor would be a better name for this option, or maybe Severe Back Strain is more appropriate. Most people don't realize it, but Yard Work is the number one source of

disabling back injuries suffered by Americans. These back injuries, however, are rarely caused by strain from work. Instead, they are usually the result of being struck from behind by a yard tool hurled at us by a howling wife as we walk down the driveway toward yet *another* fishing trip. *Helpful Tips:* Have children. They are a good source of cheap labor for those particularly demeaning yard jobs.

OPTION 4: *Fishing.* Now we're talking! Call the guys and grab the rods—it's time for some testosterone-induced, male bonding activities. You know, drillin' pigs, dirty jokes, head butts—the whole thing! *Helpful Tips:* If fishing with the guys for eight straight hours is fun, then twenty-four hours must be three times as much fun!

When you consider the options, it's no wonder many of us develop into intense, hawg-hunting maniacs. It makes perfectly good sense to me. Then again, I learned my behavior by studying the Obsessed Fisherman's official training manual: *The Old Man and the Sea.* Other people are not so understanding— like my wife, for example. Add to that list a group of brainiacs at the Nerdendork Research Center at Branedad, Texas. They conducted a study that attempts to explain why so many of us become obsessed with fishing. These brainiacs claim to have identified a

It's easy to identify an Obsessed Fisherman, just ask him a simple question:

Question: Do you like fishing?

chemical—phenylphysol—present in common fishing reel oil that is identical to the substance manufactured by the brain of an infatuated, love-struck individual. The study goes on to say that avid anglers frequently have reel oil smeared on their hands, and this chemical makes its way into the bloodstream of these unsuspecting anglers by means of skin absorption. The study concludes that obsessive fishing is, in fact, an attempt to recreate the intense feelings of past love. Furthermore, the Nerdendork pinheads insist these findings are supported by recurring reports of fishermen locked in fits of intense passion *French-kissing their baitcasting reels!* Puzzled by his unexpected behavior, one fisherman remarked, "I don't understand it, but it sure is a cheap date, and we never argue. I think it's the reel thing."

Personally, I don't believe a word of it. But I do recognize that many of us are addicted to fishing. Take me, for example: If given the choice between an intimate evening with Kim Basinger and catching the world-record bass, I'll take the trophy every time. How about you? Take the following test and see how you add up.

The Official Fishing-Addiction Test

For some people fishing is just a relaxing pastime, for others it can be a way of life—a consuming passion. Which group do you belong to? Not sure? Here are a few quick tests to help determine if you, too, are Addicted to Fishing.

Fishing Obsession Test:

☐ Do you laugh and cry during TV fishing programs?

☐ Have you ever considered using your wife's earrings as spinner-blade components?

☐ Do you ever talk to your bait?

☐ Does it ever talk back?

☐ Can you identify the fish Opie had on his stringer during the opening sequence of the "Andy of Mayberry Show"?

☐ Has your significant other ever complained about bait in the fridge?

☐ Do you direct menacing glares at jet skiers and even people you suspect may be jet skiers?

☐ Do you make fishing lists at the office when you should be working?

☐ Do you hate carp more than you hate Shiite terrorists?

☐ More than Qaddafi?

☐ More than defense lawyers? Really?

If you answered yes to any of the above, cheer up, you're not alone: Go on to the next quiz.

Would you rather ... (Be honest, now)

☐ Have sex with Kim Basinger .... ☐ Catch a world record bass

☐ Vacation in Paris .... ☐ Go on a fly-in fishing trip to Canada

☐ Get married and fish less .... ☐ Get divorced and fish more

☐ Have a meaningful conversation with your spouse. ☐ Make idle conversation with a bait-shop attendant

☐ Get promoted to big shot of the office.......... ☐ Quit your job and fish all day, every day

☐ Catch a world-record carp .... ☐ Get punched in the face by Mike Tyson

Tally ho! Add up checks from the top quiz and the right column of the bottom quiz.

☐☐ One to two boxes checked: An indication there may be cause to worry.

☐☐☐ Three to four boxes checked: Oh-oh, I would be concerned. Better monitor the situation.

☐☐☐☐☐ Five or more boxes checked: You got it bad. Join a club! Keep that line tight and proceed to the next page. Better yet, take the rest of the day off and go fishin'!

WHAT IF I SCORED 17?

I'D RATHER BE FISHING

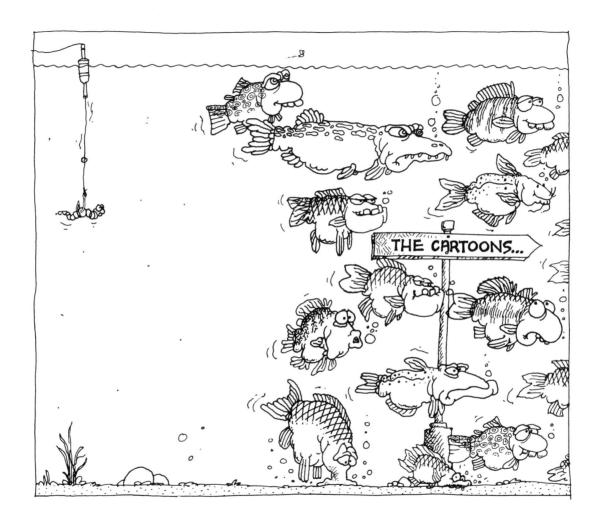

THE 8 STAGES OF GETTING SKUNKED

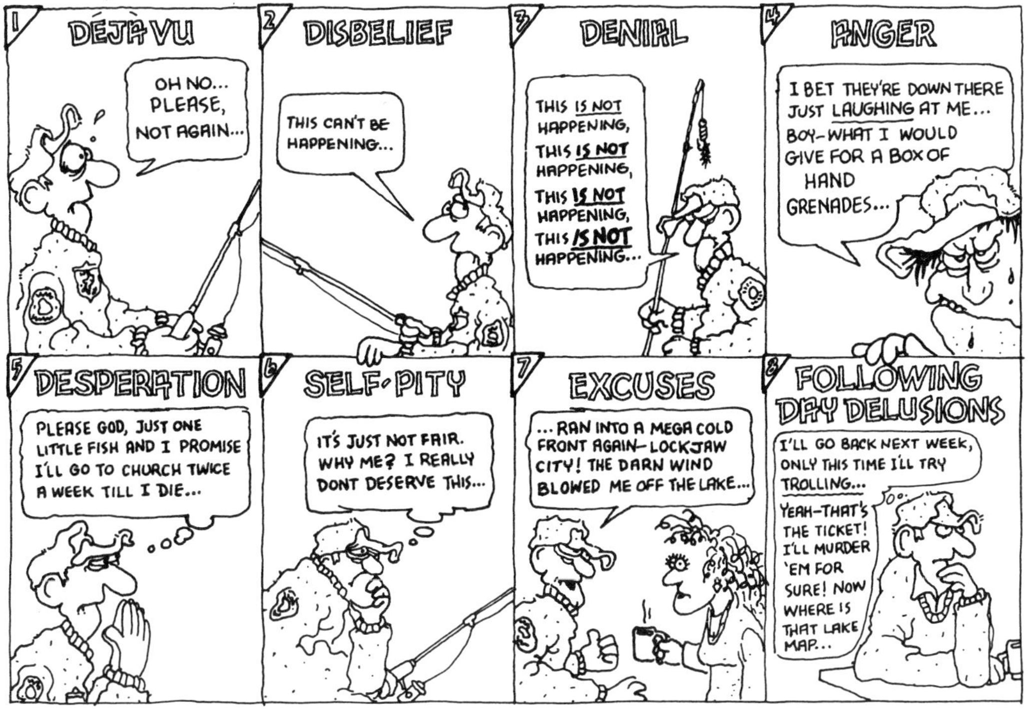

THE NEW and IMPROVED ANGLERS' GUIDE TO LIVE BAIT

TYPE OF BAIT	ADVANTAGES	DISADVANTAGES	OTHER DISADVANTAGES	FISH YOU HOPE TO CATCH USING THIS BAIT	FISH YOU WILL ACTUALLY CATCH USING THIS BAIT
NIGHTCRAWLERS	YOU CAN HAVE HOURS OF FAMILY FUN CHASING YOUR SISTERS AROUND THE HOUSE WITH THEM	THEY DIE QUICKLY	STORING WORMS IN THE FRIDGE WILL CAUSE THE LADIES IN YOUR HOUSE TO DISOWN YOU	TROUT AND ASSORTED GAME FISH	SUCKERS
MINAS	YOU'LL ALWAYS HAVE *SOME* FISH TO FRY, EVEN IF YOU GET SKUNKED	THEY DIE ON CONTACT WITH YOUR MINA BUCKET	THEY HAVE EXPRESSIVE EYES THAT LOOK AT YOU AS YOU DRIVE A HOOK THROUGH THEM	LARGEMOUTH BASS AND ASSORTED GAME FISH	BULLHEADS / TURTLES
LEECHES	ALWAYS GOOD FOR A JOKE WHEN THE FISHING IS SLOW, I.E., "OH LOOK...LUNCH"	THEY DIE THE MOMENT YOU TURN YOUR BACK	COST MORE PER POUND THAN FILET MIGNON	WALLEYE AND ASSORTED GAME FISH	CARP
CRAWFISH	YOU'LL NEVER HAVE A SLOW DAY ON THE WATER BECAUSE SHEEPS-HEAD LOVE CRAWFISH	THEY'LL USUALLY DIE IN THE CAR, ON THE WAY TO THE LAKE	THEY BITE... OFTEN	SMALLMOUTH BASS AND ASSORTED GAME FISH	SHEEPSHEAD
MAGGOTS	THERE ARE NO BENEFITS ASSOCIATED WITH MAGGOTS	THEY DIE RIGHT BEFORE YOUR VERY EYES	STORING MAGGOTS IN THE FRIDGE WILL CAUSE YOUR WIFE TO DIVORCE YOU	PANFISH	TINY SCAVENGERS
MISCELLANEOUS HELLGRAMITES WATERDOGS BEETLES SALAMANDERS SLUGS ETC.	YOU WILL GET PLENTY OF EXCERCISE CATCHING THESE BUT...	...YOU WILL PROBABLY CATCH SOME RARE DESEASE IN THE PROCESS	THEY MAY CAUSE NIGHTMARES	MISCELLANEOUS GAME FISH	MISCELLANEOUS ROUGH FISH

"OK, OK. SO IT'S POURING FOR THE FIFTH STRAIGHT
WEEKEND, THAT'S NO REASON TO GO OFF THE DEEP END."

FERGY FINALLY CATCHES A TROPHY.

GEORGE TRIED TO CREATE A SUPERIOR BAIT BY ADDING
STEROIDS TO HIS WORM FARM...

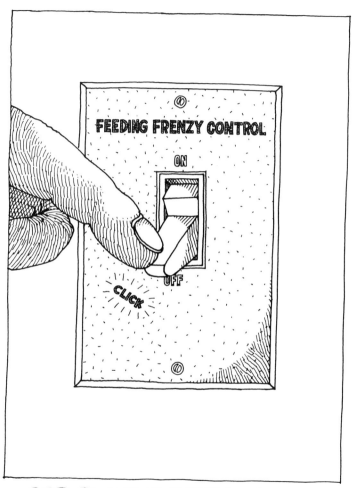

GOD PLAYING DIRTY TRICKS

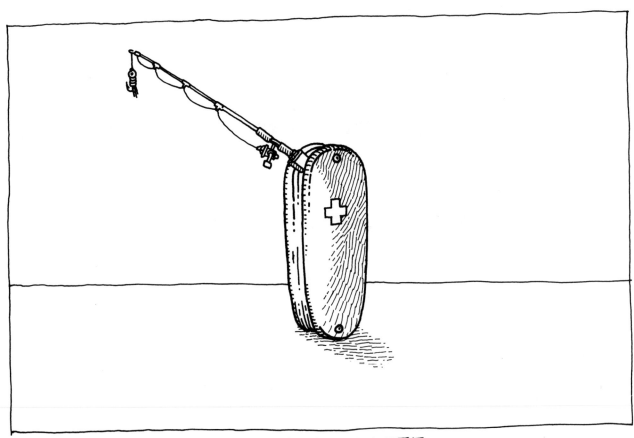

SWISS ARMY KNIFE
WITH MY KIND OF ATTACHMENT.

MY KIND OF MACY'S THANKSGIVING PARADE.

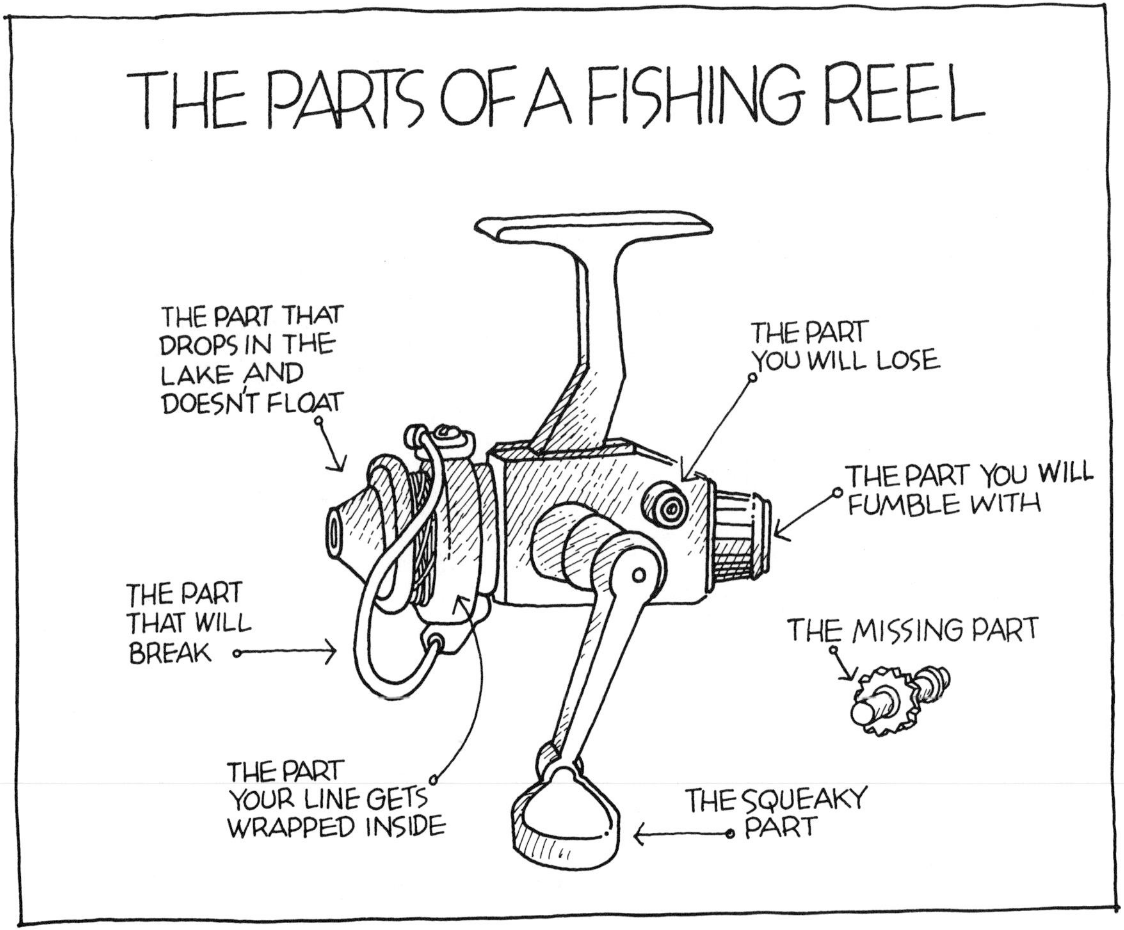

THE PARTS OF A FISHING REEL

THE PART THAT DROPS IN THE LAKE AND DOESN'T FLOAT

THE PART YOU WILL LOSE

THE PART YOU WILL FUMBLE WITH

THE PART THAT WILL BREAK

THE MISSING PART

THE PART YOUR LINE GETS WRAPPED INSIDE

THE SQUEAKY PART

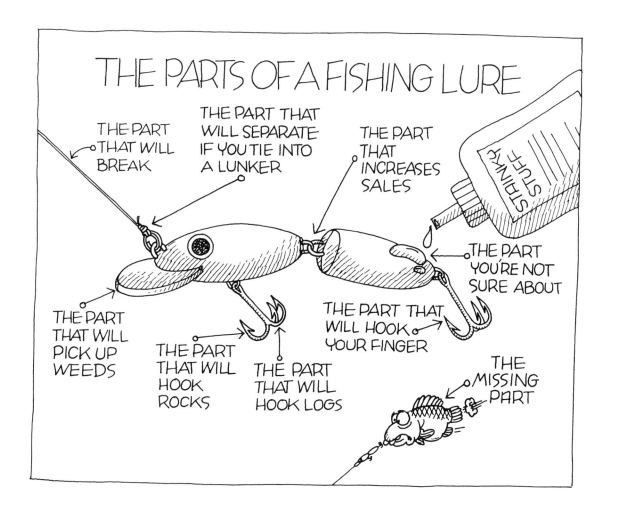

THE PARTS OF A FISHING LURE

THE PART THAT WILL BREAK

THE PART THAT WILL SEPARATE IF YOU TIE INTO A LUNKER

THE PART THAT INCREASES SALES

STINKY STUFF

THE PART YOU'RE NOT SURE ABOUT

THE PART THAT WILL PICK UP WEEDS

THE PART THAT WILL HOOK ROCKS

THE PART THAT WILL HOOK LOGS

THE PART THAT WILL HOOK YOUR FINGER

THE MISSING PART

"MANY FISH COMING, KEMO SABE. TEN, MEBBE TWELVE HOGS."

The Passionate Angler—Heaven or Hell?

There are advantages to being an Avid Angler. For one, you have a socially acceptable excuse to shirk most adult responsibilities. Also, bait-shop cashiers will greet you by name, which is easy for them to remember because it is etched on their brain from having cleared your credit card three times a week for the past ten fishing seasons. Another terrific benefit is that you will eventually become a walking fishing encyclopedia, quoting from volumes of useless information gleaned from countless magazine articles written about obscure subjects, like Downrigging on Western Reservoirs. Or my personal favorite: Effective Jigging Techniques for Use During Low-Light, Cold-Front, Slightly Intoxicated Conditions. Only when we discover we are mouthing the words of the article before we actually come to them do we realize we have been reading basically the same eight universal articles written and rewritten over and over by different authors in different magazines. But hey—inquiring minds want to know.

There are disadvantages, too. For starters, the high cost of lures will eventually wipe out your total annual family income, including loose change that fell down into the couch. Here's another disadvantage you might want to mull over while sharpening hooks tonight. Upon death, you will certainly go to minnow hell for the killing and maiming of countless innocent minnows. And last, but not least, are the unmanageable problems that develop from neglect—specifically, the neglect of one's family and household duties. These problems are unavoidable for the passionate angler. Fortunately, there is a solution. What I do about these problems is basically the same thing I do about *all* life's nagging problems—namely, I try not to think about them and go fishing instead.

38

THE SIX STAGES OF A FISHING DAY

THE ANGLER'S GUIDE TO GAMEFISH PERSONALITY TRAITS

SPECIES	DOMINANT PERSONALITY TRAIT	SECONDARY PERSONALITY TRAIT	LIKES	DISLIKES	TECHNIQUE MOST LIKELY TO PUT 'EM IN THE BOAT
LARGEMOUTH BASS	DIFFICULT TO CATCH	ELUSIVE STUBBORN/ WON'T BITE	LIKES TO SPIT THE HOOK AT BOAT SIDE	EVERY LURE IN YOUR TACKLE BOX	HAND GRENADES
WALLEYE	IMPOSSIBLE TO CATCH	SECRETIVE PARANOID/ WON'T BITE	LOVES TO PICK UP BAIT AND DROP IT TILL YOU GO CRAZY	LEMON AND BUTTER	SPEARGUN
BIG NORTHERN PIKE	IMPOSSIBLE TO CATCH. YOU'RE BETTER OFF FISHING FOR FRIGGIN' MERMAIDS	RECLUSIVE/ WON'T BITE	LIKES TO TEAR AT FINGERS PLACED CARELESSLY CLOSE TO MASSIVE JAWS	EVERYTHING THAT MOVES	DANGLE BARE TOES IN THE WATER... **CAUTION:** *REMAIN ALERT!*
BROWN TROUT	RARELY CATCHABLE	SKITTISH EASILY SPOOKED/ WON'T BITE	LOVES TO EMBARRASS OVER ACCESSORIZED FLY FISHERMEN	BARELY PERCEPTIBLE SOUNDS AND MOVEMENTS, SUCH AS BREATHING AND BLINKING	VELVEETA/ KERNEL CORN TREBLE HOOK TREATS
CRAPPIE	THEY'RE CATCHABLE, BUT FIRST YOU GOTTA FIND THEM.	NOMADIC, UNPREDICTABLE/ WON'T BITE	THE ONE JIG YOU DECIDED TO LEAVE AT HOME	EVERY BAIT IN YOUR POSSESSION	SONAR AND DYNAMITE
CHANNEL CATFISH	OCCASIONALLY CATCHABLE BUT DON'T COUNT ON IT	OCCASIONALLY COOPERATIVE/ OTHERWISE WON'T BITE	STAINKY STUFF	BEER BATTER	ANTI-SUBMARINE DEPTH CHARGES
CARP	ANNOYINGLY EASY TO CATCH, COUNT ON IT	ANNOYINGLY COOPERATIVE/ ALWAYS BITE	WONDERBREAD, OLD TWINKIE WRAPPERS	THE GAFF, THE BOOT, ORIENTALS	ALL TECHNIQUES ARE ANNOYINGLY EFFECTIVE

40

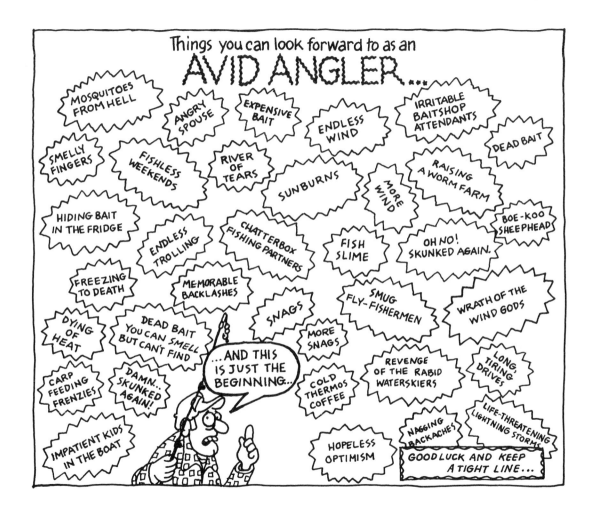

HANK GIVES HIS LIVE BAIT A PEP TALK
ON THE EVE OF THE BIG FISHING TRIP.

ELMER EXPERIENCES A LITTLE STATIC IN THE ATTIC.

45

ONCE AGAIN, WAYNE FLASHES THAT SMUG, CHIDING GRIN
AS HE RUNS UP THE CRAPPIE SCORE 15-O.

46

REALIZING HE HAS NO CHANCE AT WINNING THE
BASS TOURNAMENT, DWAYNE PLAYS THE ROLE OF SPOILER.

47

"I CHANGED MY MIND... LET'S BET ON THE **BIGGEST** FISH INSTEAD OF THE **MOST** FISH."

"I NEVER HEARD OF POURING FISH SCENT RIGHT INTO THE WATER, THINK IT'LL WORK?"

"IN TIMES LIKE THESE YOU FIND OUT IF YOU'RE BASICALLY FANATICAL OR NOT."

Carp! The Fish That Lacks Credibility

It's interesting that the same God who created cutthroat trout and smallmouth bass also created carp. That Big Guy Upstairs . . . what a kidder.

I'll never forget the time my buddy was hauling in what he thought was a trophy walleye. He was so excited over the strength of the fish, he started babbling like some Arab street merchant cranked on helium. I can still see his face smiling from ear to ear. Suddenly, the smile vanished. His face was stricken with a dazed, perplexed expression, like a starved Ethiopian just handed a piece of wax fruit. I looked overboard and saw why. It wasn't a walleye at all. It was a huge, disgusting carp.

Angling addicts hate carp because . . . well, because they're carp. You can't really blame them, there's not a whole lot to like. Basically, the Carp Man has three prominent characteristics:

An extremely dim IQ: no Mensa candidates here. As a matter of fact, the only living organism with less measurable brain activity than a carp was found hanging under a dank, moldy public washroom sink somewhere in Newark, New Jersey—in the form of a severely retarded cockroach. However, what Mr. Carp lacks in brain power, he more than makes up for with amazing food-finding instincts. The Institute for Obtaining Absurd Public Grants discovered that only moments after birth, a carp will swim straight for the bottom, where it will wander tirelessly, traveling hundreds of miles if necessary, until it locates its primary food source: a worm on a hook.

Once the C-Man locates the focus of his intense desires—live bait—he will practice his second prominent characteristic:

Sucking stuff in: we're talking world-class vacuum cleaner here folks . . . *power lips*! Those highly developed lip muscles are so strong, the C-Man can literally inhale a full-grown crawler from fifty feet—*against the current*! In fact, there have been cases

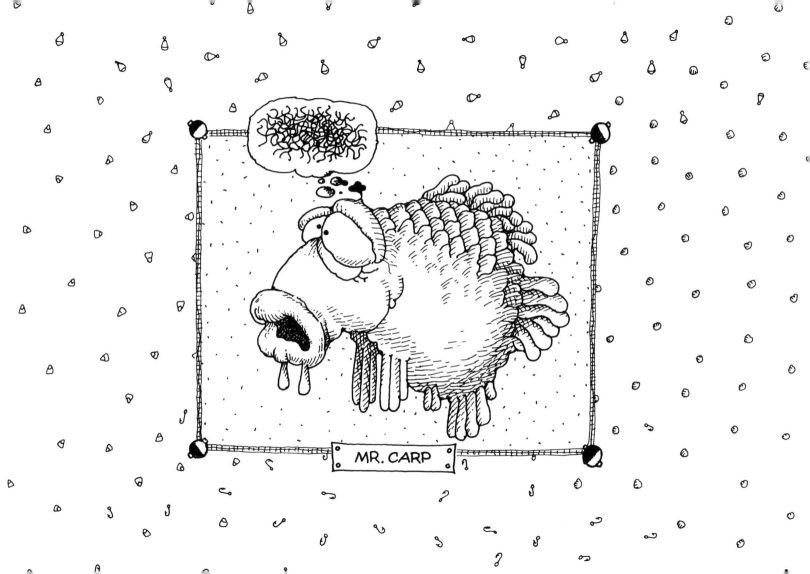

reported of carp skeletons, permanently attached by the mouth to underwater rocks. Apparently, the C-Man can turn on a *power suck* so ferocious in intensity, he can become permanently welded to rock.

At this very moment, the Hoover Vacuum Corporation has a research-and-development team feverishly working around the clock, trying to unlock the secrets to the *power suck* for possible future patent rights.

It is a known fact that Mr. C will inhale *anything* that falls in the path of his rubbery Hoovers. Including all forms of toxic sludge, which brings us to prominent characteristic number three:

Carp are glo-hounds: I, personally, have never had my fingernails ripped out, but I have seen it dramatized in a Rambo movie, and believe me, it's not a pretty sight. However, I would rather experience a severe denailing, including all ten toes, than eat one fork full of carp meat. Especially after reading about a New York research team that examined the stomach contents of a Love Canal carp. They were absolutely astonished by their findings: Vaseline-smeared beer cans, globs of highly toxic industrial waste, and enough radioactive sludge to light up downtown Buffalo from now until Christmas!

All that glo-food might help to explain the bizarre carp-related incidents that have taken place in New York City. Apparently their sewer system is becoming badly infested with extremely aggressive and highly unpredictable Glo-Carp. Recently, some of the fish have found their way into the public plumbing system. A frightened New Yorker described a recent carp encounter as "spookier than a Geraldo show, although not quite as long."

FRIGHTENED NEW YORKER: "I was sitting on the throne, minding my own business, when all of a sudden, something *really gooey* locked onto my left cheek! It felt as if I was being sucked down into the toilet by a giant plunger. And that sound . . . *ugh!* I will *never* forget that *gurgling* sound as long as I live. It was *disgusting*! I felt . . . violated!"

Believe it or not, there was once a time when America was Carp-Free. It's incredible to think that all those carp originated from five sickly little Sludge-buckets imported from China, via Germany, in 1872.

Every time I catch one of those little Hoovers, I get highly P.O.'d because I can practically visualize a nasty little label on its bloated belly that says: Made in China. Well, I have a solution. I say we send the little Hoovers back where they came from! Let's gather up all those Slimebellies, cram them into one big, South Dakota missile silo and launch the little Dung Demons straight back to Tiananmen Square! Like, you know, an Intercontinental Carp Missile. *Hold the phone* . . . I have a better idea! I say we load up one of those super tankers until it's bursting at the seams with carp and . . . hell, while we're at it, let's trash *all* our surplus vermin! Let's stuff Imelda Marcos in there and the ol' Ice Queen herself—Leona Helmsley. We could even add any defense lawyers who have successfully defended rapists, murderers, or major corporations during the last ten years. Uh, better make that two tankers. We'll pack 'em all onto the *Valdez* and point that sucker straight toward Beijing. Provide an open bar for the crew,. and before long . . . CRASH! "Hey whad the . . . *hic!* . . . this ain't Alazzzka . . . *hic!* . . . whar the hell are we? . . . *hic!*"

Try to understand me, it's not that I don't like carp. I do. They serve a very important purpose in life—namely, to suck rocks and gill-filter mud. However, I will *never* consider carp as a gamefish. To me, fishing for carp would be like hunting dairy cows with a high-powered rifle and scope. In fact, the thought of catching a limit of carp— Wait a minute—there is no such thing as a limit of carp. Anyway, the thought of *intentionally* catching *any* carp is so repulsive to me, I would rather catch a rare skin disease and wind up with a General Noriega pizza face, than intentionally catch a stringer of Hoovers.

Not that I have a choice. You can't avoid the little bait robbers, but at least we can determine how bad the infestation is:

GLUDDD SLODDSHH SLURRP SLURRDOLL GLOSSSHERDD

Carp Infestation Test

- Dangle a juicy crawler six inches above the water. If carp immediately school beneath it making sucking gestures toward the bait, the water is EXTREMELY INFESTED.
- Lower the bait six inches below the surface. If a carp inhales the bait within ten seconds, the water is MODERATELY INFESTED.
- Sink the bait to the bottom with a heavy weight. If you catch only three carp within three minutes, the water is LIGHTLY INFESTED. Be thankful. That's as good as it gets.

What we are up against here is a situation that has confounded American bait fishermen for over a century: "How do I keep those sludgebuckets offa my friggin' bait? Can't someone *do something* about them?" Well, not exactly. But here are some helpful tips that may help you to avoid the Carp Man:

Useful Carp-Deterrent Tips

- Soak your bait in a solution of one part Cutter's Insect Repellent and two parts nail polish remover. Rinse well with ice water and drizzle lightly with English Leather. This will keep the carp *offa your friggin' bait* for approximately thirty-seven seconds.
- Next time you're at the bait shop, make sure you try the new Carp-Free Crawlers. That way you are sure to catch *less* than one-thousand of the little scumbellies.
- Try switching baits. I have a friend who fishes Lake Erie and swears by crayfish: "If them Hoovers get too frisky, I just switch to crabs." Surprisingly enough, this method actually works! You won't catch any carp, but only because they can't get near your crawfish, which will be surrounded by thousands of rabid sheepheads tearing it apart.

When all else fails, at least you can enjoy some comic relief by practicing the catch-and-release methods recommended in the *Carp Haters of the World (C.H.O.W.) Handbook*:

The Babe Ruth Method: Most C.H.O.W. Hounds recommend that you keep a Louisville Slugger on board for those *special moments*.

The Doctor Ruth Method: Chatter incessantly at the poor fish in a playful, whiny little voice until its brain dissolves into goo. Toss overboard.

The End-Zone Spike: Have fun using the deck of your boat as an imaginary end zone and spike that Bulge Belly! Go ahead —take the "tacked-on yardage penalty" by doing a steroid-induced end-zone dance after each spike! It's worth it!

C.H.O.W., baby. Catch ya later!

Remember, in some states it's against the law to release a Rubber Lip alive. You may want to consider more drastic measures. You may want to consider the ZERO TOLERANCE METHODS as described in the *Young Urban Carp Killers Inc. (Y.U.C.K.I.) Handbook:*

Zero-Tolerance Carp-Disposal Methods

The Cranial Aerator: Keep a cordless Black & Decker handy and drill Mr. C. a fresh porthole—right between the eyes. It's a Y.U.C.K.I. fave!

The Chinese Teapot: This is stage two of the Cranial Aerator. Cover the C-Man's pouting nostrils and blow really hard into his mouth. Hey, all right . . . it whistles! What you have created here is a highly effective Carp Whistle o' Warning that *all* Hoovers understand *and fear.*

The Pigskin Space Shuttle: drop-kick that bulgebelly, NFL style, for three points. Hint: Steel tips will improve your hangtime dramatically.

The Rambo Lob: Jam a cherry bomb in his trap and *hit the deck!*

The Freddy Krueger Method: Y.U.C.K.I.s affectionately refer to this method as "Doin' the Freddie." Use your imagination.

(If you think I'm being a little rough on the C-Man, keep this in mind: This is probably the most sensitive and caring passage ever written on the subject of Carp Disposal.)

Does catching a carp bring on a raging mood swing? Would you kill to rid your favorite waters of this bothersome bait grabber? Do you feel powerless over the situation? Well, maybe it's time to stop your carping and *do* something about it! Strap on your six-shooters, grab your Yippee-Yi-Yo-Ki-Yay hat and join the C.H.O.W. Hounds! Take this quick test to find out if you are indeed C.H.O.W. material:

The Carp Haters of the World
ELIGIBILITY TEST

Answer the following questions as honestly as possible.

1. **You think people who fish for carp are:**
   a. open-minded
   b. making the best of a bad situation
   c. *very* sick individuals

2. **When you hear the word "carp," which image springs to mind?**
   a. lemon and butter
   b. sucking lips
   c. your last bowel movement

3. **You consider carp to be:**
   a. a gamefish
   b. a rough fish
   c. a dead fish, if you can help it

4. **In your opinion, carp should be:**
   a. tolerated
   b. controlled
   c. hunted down
      and destroyed

5. **If you *had* to eat one of the following, you would choose:**
   a. carp
   b. roadkill
   c. Drano

6. **If someone told you that your favorite fast-food fishwich was, in fact, carp, you would:**
   a. thank him for the information
   b. gag
   c. kill the messenger

7. After finding out that your favorite fast-food restaurant was secretly serving you carp, you would:
   a. stop eating there
   b. stop eating there and send the manager a letter of complaint
   c. stop eating there and send the manager a letter bomb

8. When you catch a carp, the first thing you usually say is:
   a. "quick, hand me the stringer"
   b. "quick, hand me the net"
   c. "quick, hand me the hatchet"

9. When you catch a carp, your friends usually:
   a. congratulate you
   b. crack corny jokes about your fishing skills
   c. crack dirty jokes about your mother

10. After landing a carp, your fishing partner usually gives you:
    a. high fives
    b. a poke in the ribs and a wink
    c. a poke in the eye with a sharp stick

11. Your solution to the carp problem would be:
    a. to tolerate them
    b. to grin and bear it
    c. to declare Holy War

12. If you caught the world-record carp, you would:
    a. take pictures, then release the fish unharmed
    b. keep the fish and have it mounted
    c. kill the Fat Sludgebucket and mount the weapon

KEY

If you answered "a" to six or more questions, you obviously don't meet the c.h.o.w. membership standards. You might want to try Carp Unlimited. They have a reputation for accepting degenerate sickos like yourself.

If you answered "b" to six or more questions, you don't quite make the grade. You might want to try The Society of Fence Sitters, or possibly the Democratic Party. Good luck.

If you answered "c" to six or more questions, congratulations! I'll bet this is the first test you've passed since taking the Armed Texans Against Eastern Liberals entrance exam. Just scratch your mark on the dotted line and we'll send you the Official c.h.o.w. Starter Kit, which includes your very own monogrammed Louisville Slugger, a dozen cherry bombs, and the official .h.o.w. shoulder patch.

c.h.o.w., baby . . . catch ya later!

The Carpin' Corner

Bobby Joe Brainded

Willy Gumbo

TIP #21 — TIPS FOR CARP LOVERS

CANNED CORN VS. FROZEN

"Give me frozen anyday! She'll stay on the hook longer and those frisky little critters sure like a cool treat on a hot summer day! I like to set 'er out in the sun till she ripens up **real good**. Then I freeze 'er up solid. She'll set on that hook for a good two-three hours. U-m-m-m-m boy— heaven on a hook!"

TIP #37 — TIPS FOR CARP HATERS

CATCH AND RELEASE TACTICS

"I like to release carp with an overhand lob onto shore. If i'm too far from land, then I release them with a baseball bat, or sometimes i'll just release them with the butt of my fillet knife."

Well there you have it sports fans... love 'em or leave 'em, toss 'em or eat 'em... either way – they'll have to pay.

IN BOX DEPT...

Thanks to Bobo Rodriguez from Nohope, New Jersy for sending in this idea for a *very unique* bird feeder.

Way to go Bobo!

DID YOU KNOW...

◆ A recent study claims that cigar butts and stale Doritos are near the top of the list of favorite carp snacks. The treat that topped the list?.. Chee-tos dipped in valve sealant, of course. Aren't you glad you asked?

◆ Three out of four carp prefer whole wheat to white.

◆ Recent field tests indicate that an average sized carp will flop 17-21 times after being lobbed up onto shore.

NEXT WEEK: The incredible glow carp of Lake Chernobyl

ORGANIZERS OF THE FIRST ANNUAL CARP COOK-OFF RUN INTO
A MAJOR OBSTACLE—NO ONE IS WILLING TO JUDGE THE ENTRIES.

THE GUYS OVER AT THE PINE TREE
FISHING RESORT **LOVE** A GOOD GAME OF CARPS.

"NO, YOU DON'T UNDERSTAND, **_WE PAY YOU_** $50 TO JOIN."

THE CRIME: TAKING TOO MUCH TIME ON THE BOAT RAMP.
THE PUNISHMENT: DEATH BY CARP.

A CONCERNED CITIZEN CHECKING THE I.D. OF A SUSPICIOUS LOOKING CARP.

MAGAZINES
I'D LIKE TO SEE...

73

Wouldn't It Be Great If the Whole World Were Addicted to Fishing?

I was having one of those dismal days on the water when the insect-bite-to-fish-bite ratio was about thirty thousand to one. You know the type of day I'm talking about, the kind that, if you were *forced* to endure, would be called torture. But since you are there *voluntarily*, it's called fishing. Anyway, delirium must have set in sometime after my ninety-seventh involuntary blood donation. Because a crazy question popped into my head and wouldn't go away: *What if the whole world were*

THE MOSQUITO TURBIN

addicted to fishing? What if the whole friggin' planet fished with a fanaticism that made a Shiite terrorist, hell bent for Holy War, seem timid by comparison?

No doubt about it, the world would become . . . *A Special Place.*

Imagine the demand 5 billion angling addicts would create for fishing products. I bet the ripple effect would change the world! Hell, it might even change that Mecca of excessive consumerism, THE GIGANTIC SUBURBAN SUPERMARKET. Gigantic supermarket executives would probably invent some hot new consumer attractions like: THE BULK BAIT SECTION. Picture it. Aisle after aisle, stacked to the rafters with BAIT BARRELS, just squirming with farm-fresh crawlers. Grade A, foot-long, jumbo jumpers by the scoop!

The gigantic marketing department would probably have a collective orgasm creating—just what the world

74

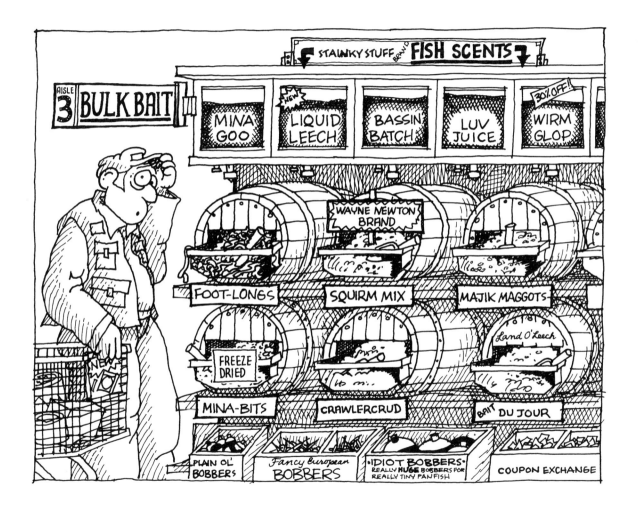

needs—one more very forgettable TV commercial. Of course, it would feature some GROSSLY OVERPAID ATHLETE who is paid more per day than the gross national product of most third world nations. He would land a fish, turn to face the camera, and read some ridiculously simplistic line:

GROSSLY OVERPAID ATHLETE: (*to camera*) "Bo knows bait."

TOTALLY STRESSED-OUT ADVERTISING EXEC: "Love it! That's a wrap. Let's do lunch!"

Of course, no commercial would be complete without a catchy jingle. Right after the famous jock reads his line, an obnoxious song will kick in, complete with Lite And Happy Music:

♪ *Ever-squirm Worms, the bait fish love to bite.*

These catchy little melodies have a very sinister objective: to eat away at your brain like little carnivorous corkscrews until you run screaming to the gigantic suburban supermarket, clutching your open wallet in hand, begging them to take your money, take your firstborn, take anything—but please, *oh, please* take that relentless broken record out of your head before it explodes like some sort of cranial jack-in-the-box, right there in the store!

My delirium was intensifying. I was imagining I was in Bulk Bait Heaven, steering my wobbly wheeled shopping cart through the generic freeze-dried mina section, and reciting the "Lord Have Mercy on the Man with Three Carts Full" prayer, when, suddenly it occurred to me, the real reason people subject themselves to this bizarre weekly routine is not because they need to buy *food* but because they need an *excuse* to buy *The National Enquirer.*

If the whole world had a fishing fetish, that would add up to one hefty target audience with an itch just dying to be scratched. It wouldn't take long before rabid reporters directed their hyper-attention toward the fishing world:

FAMOUS JOCK COLLECTS ASTRONOMICAL FEE FOR BAIT COMMERCIAL—BUYS YUGOSLAVIA
"It's a pretty cool place, you know, with all them onion domes 'n' shit? So I bought it."

WOMAN GIVES BIRTH TO 12-LB. CARP WHILE DRIVING BUS!
Love child has father's lips . . .

Liz Pleads:
"MARTIANS IN MY MINNOW BUCKET!"
"Make them go away . . ."

WOMAN KILLS HUBBY OVER LAST MINNOW!
"It was mine and he knew it. So I killed the bastard!"

Minnesota Mom Begs:
ALIEN STURGEON ATE MY BABY!
"Please help me find him before it's too late! He's the one with the large bulge in his belly."

Once the tabloids jump on the fishing bandwagon, TV won't be far behind. Wouldn't it be wild to see a fishing sitcom on TV? I can see it now—*The Cass Tandfa t Show*. Featuring—just what the world needs—two more FAT SITCOM STARS. Now *that* would be funny. Or would it? Let's face it, most sitcoms are about as funny as a root canal.

I wouldn't want to give you the wrong impression: I *like* sitcoms. Some of them are even funny. Besides, they serve a very valuable purpose—namely, to fill the 5-minute gaps between commercials.

Fishing tabloids. Fishing Sitcoms. Fishing Records . . . this *must* be Fishing Heaven. The huge recording companies would flood the airwaves with trendy music.

Everything from heavy metal bands with articulate names like The Dead Minas, to catfishing rap bands—e.g., Catmandoo and the Inner City Kitties. Boomboxes blaring Cat Rap songs might even become commonplace:

You take some funky chicken livers
an' you wrap it on your hook.
Wrap it good 'n' tight, so's a frisky little kitty
won't take the bait 'n' book.

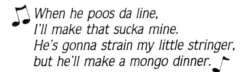
Wrap that liver,
it's a real cat killer.
It brings 'em up from the bottom—
I know, because I caught 'em.

When he poos da line,
I'll make that sucka mine.
He's gonna strain my little stringer,
but he'll make a mongo dinner.

Boomboxes and Cat Rap music? That brings up the likelihood that Fishing Heaven might have a dark side. Maybe it wouldn't be all fun and games. Maybe if the whole world was addicted to fishing, the whole world would also be highly P.O.'d at things like crowded fishing holes. Then again, that could just be nature's way of Thinning the Herd. Especially in California, where tormented drivers think nothing of blowing each other away over minor traffic infractions:

APOLOGETIC FISHERMAN: (*as he crosses another angler's line*) "Looks like we're tangled. Sorry."
TORMENTED ANGLER: (*pulling up a sawed-off shotgun*) "Bad move, scumbag—EAT LEAD AND DIE!"

Maybe if we all fished, the world would become a smaller place. After all, who would have guessed the Iron Curtain would fall as fast as it did. It was just a short time ago that Lech Walesa was quoted as saying, "If the borders of Poland are ever opened, will the last person out please turn off the lights and close the windows?" I suppose it's inevitable that someone will start some kind of Fishing Foreign Exchange Program. Can you imagine a group of Polish fishermen arriving in Texas for a week of bass fishing, "Good Ol' Boy" style?

GOOD OL' BOY: (*fingering coins in his pockets*) "So what kinda bass boats you boys got over there in Poland?"
POLISH ANGLER: (*gaping*) "Bess bots? What is bess bots please?"
GOOD OL' BOY: "No, not bess bots—Bass Boats ... BASS BOATS!"

POLISH ANGLER: "Ahhh, passports. I have such a blue passport, thank you."
GOOD OL' BOY: "No, not *passports*. Piss Pots ... I mean Biss Box ... Oh Sweet Jesus! Forget it. Let's go have a beer!"

There's no telling how much the world would be affected. Some of it good, some bad. Of course, there would be those things that fall in between, things you don't know what to make of, like suburban fishing malls:

BESS BOTS? WHAT IS BESS BOTS PLEASE?

78

REEL WORLD

The world's largest mall devoted entirely to fishing.
(Directory of stores and services)

Level 1: Live Bait

Ernie's Earthworm Emporium: *Don't pick them, pick us.*

Squirmin' Thurmon's Wormin' World: *You're gonna think you died and went to Live Bait Heaven!*

The Maggot Man: *Ask about our "Majik Maggot."*

Willie's Warehouse o' Worms: *Home of the Foot-Long.*

Level 2: Tackle Stores

Bobbers "R" Us: *One-stop shopping for all your bobber needs. Visit our showroom—you'll be glad you did.*

Lenny's Lures and Loans: *We'll take your money, then we'll lend you more.*

Gumbo Willie's Hooker Haven: *We'll put the glom on you.*

NameCo: *Formerly JimCo, JohnCo, and JoeCo. The Tackle to Go-Co.*

Level 3: Fly-Fishing Stores

The Compleat Anglo: *Fine fly-fishing apparel that will make you look like a preppy jerk.*

The Snob Shop: *Expensive tackle for purist fly fishermen who think spending money will make them better anglers.*

Level 4: Miscellaneous Services

Fibber, Lyer, and Sneek, Angling Attorneys at Law: *Lining our pockets since 1973.*

Smith, Blarney, Angling Investors: *We make money the old-fashioned way . . . by insider trading.*

Acme Plumbing and Guide Service: *Watch your fishing troubles go down the drain.*

During our fishing careers, we all experience periods when no matter how hard we try, we just can't get out and go fishing. It's during these dry spells that the Hard Core experience a behavioral phenomenon known as "Fishing Withdrawal Syndrome." It starts as a tight feeling around the collar and gradually progresses to a raging emotional disorder. Anglers! Know the enemy! FWS may be draining your energies at this very moment. Take the following quiz and see how you measure up.

The Fishing-Withdrawal Syndrome Quiz

Answer the following questions as honestly as you can. If you find them too personal or frightening, you've probably already failed.

1. During long, fishless periods you catch yourself:
   a. arguing with your spouse

b. arguing with your boss

c. arguing with your mina bucket

2. Depression, caused by FWS, prevents you from:
   a. getting to work on time
   b. taking proper care of your bait farm
   c. interacting with the other patients

3. It's been a long, long time since you last fished. On the eve of the big fishing trip you:
   a. stay up till midnight sharpening hooks
   b. practice fish cleaning by filleting every guppy in the aquarium
   c. get in a little hooksetting practice by trolling for neighborhood cats off the back of your pickup

4. It's been six dismal weeks since you last wet a line. Finally, the big day comes. You arrive at the boat ramp only to find a long line caused by a slow, elderly couple. You:
   a. patiently wait your turn
   b. organize a lynch mob
   c. introduce them to the Uzi School of Dancing

5. During one unusually long fishless period, you became irritable and were fired from your job because:
   a. you forgot office protocol and frequently disagreed with management
   b. you forgot that you are not supposed to punch out your boss
   c. you forgot where the hell the office was

6. During long fishless periods, your coworkers notice a change in your behavior and consider you to be:
   a. a little impatient
   b. really strange
   c. a ticking bomb

7. Your secretary neglects to give you an important telephone message from your best fishing buddy. You:
   a. gently reprimand her
   b. call her a tramp and fire her
   c. interrogate her with a bright light and an electric prod

8. You catch your children playing in your tackle box. You:
   a. send them to their room
   b. send them to their room gagged and bound in straitjackets
   c. bury their remains under the house

9. You lost your fillet knife during a mental funk caused by FWS. Later that week, you find it:
   a. in the medicine cabinet
   b. stuck in a wall
   c. buried in the back of the guy that sold you dead crawlers

10. The waiter gave you regular coffee instead of decaf. You:
   a. leave a lousy tip
   b. stay up till midnight organizing your tackle box
   c. lie awake all night wondering who else is out to get you

I CAN IDENTIFY WITH THAT STUFF...

YUCK!

KEY

If you answered "a" to five or more questions, you are clearly unaffected by fishless periods. However, some people consider that in itself to be pretty strange behavior.

If you answered "b" to five or more questions, your reaction to fishless periods is pretty much normal. Your fear that alien beings are sending you messages through your depth finder must be the result of some other behavioral disorder.

If you answered heavy on the "c's," there's no doubt about it—you have a full-blown, raging FWS. If you go any length of time without fishing you become, you know, like, totally mental. Fortunately, there is a cure. Fishing and lots of it! Now if we could only get the health insurance companies to pay for the treatment . . .

WOULDN'T IT BE WILD TO SEE A TV FISHING SITCOM,
COMPLETE WITH FAT TV STARS?

WOULDN'T IT BE REALLY GREAT IF THE WHOLE WORLD WERE ADDICTED TO FISHING? WE WOULD HAVE THINGS LIKE, BAIT AND TACKLE COMMERCIALS...
NATE'S
YES-SIREEE BOB. HURRY ON DOWN TO NATE'S NIGHTCRAWLER CLEARANCE WAREHOUSE, WE'LL TREAT YOU LIKE A BIG FISH.
3

WOULDN'T IT BE GREAT IF THE WHOLE WORLD WERE ADDICTED TO FISHING?
WE WOULD HAVE THINGS LIKE, *CATFISHING RAP MUSIC...*

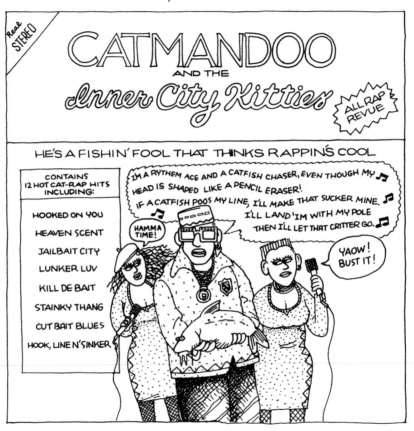

Marital Blitz!

Marriage is a great experience, I highly recommend it, even to fishing maniacs like myself. Unfortunately, most people think avid angling and happily married are conflicting terms. A happy fishing marriage can be achieved if, and only if, you understand the Three Basic Principles of Marriage. They are:

PRINCIPLE #1. Husbands and wives view *everything* from such *totally* different perspectives you'd think they were born on different planets.

PRINCIPLE #2. Marriage is not a catch-and-release program. Its survival depends on how well you master the Two Essential Marriage Skills: Lying and Arguing.

PRINCIPLE #3. Marriage, Change, and the Irritant Factor will suck your brain dry.

PRINCIPLE #1. Husbands and wives view *everything* from such *totally* different perspectives, you'd think they were born on different planets.

Eventually, the thrill of dating fades and you will be faced with the one question that, sooner or later, confronts all couples: Should we break up, or should we get married? If you decide she's a keeper and are determined to tie the knot of marital bliss . . . Yo! Congratulations and high-fives all around! However, there is one thing you should keep in mind: Members of the opposite sex view *everything* from *totally* different perspectives. I'm talking *radically* different worlds here! Take for example, the word "Vacation." I would fly north. Katherine would fly south. She would kill for a hot, crowded, fashion-statement beach while I dream of clear northern lakes that run cold and deep, the way God intended. As you might expect, vacation planning at our house can get a little

confrontational. As a matter of fact, sometimes it resembles twelve rounds of Wrestlemania! "In this corner . . . Katherine the Fashion Fascist, weighing in at 122 pounds (plus 4 pounds of lead pipe clenched between her teeth), vs. Georgio the Fishing Ninja and his Stringer-O'-Death!" This event usually ends when one of us shrieks *"Give! I'd love to do it your way!"* Most years we never do get away. We can't afford it. Our vacation funds are usually wasted replacing broken furniture.

That reminds me of a situation that occurred at the mall. A pair of earrings caught my wife's attention and she held them up for my opinion. They were black with triangle-shaped blades. Naturally, I gave them a two-thumbs-down, and pointed to a silver pair with oval-shaped blades. I explained, "These babies will attract far more strikes and work better during most light conditions. All you need is a weedless hook and we're talkin' *Hawg City*!" I even offered to go halves if she promised to let me use them on weekends. Needless to say, we don't shop for earrings together anymore.

Helpful Hint: Pick up a copy of *Married Angler Magazine*. It's just loaded with lip-rippin', jaw-jerkin', marriage-saving articles like:

- Five Great Fishing Articles to Read While Your Wife Is in Labor
- It's Summer. Do You Know Where Your Husband Is?
- Ten Hot New Lures and How They can Ruin Your Marriage
- Fishing on Christmas: How to Get Away with It
- Full Stringer, Empty Arms: Too Much Fishing and Not Enough Lovin'
- Sex: My, How She Loves That Flippin' Stick!
- Men Who Fish: Husbands with Halos or Husbands with Horns?
- Hormonal Horror Stories: I Had a PMS Vampire in the Boat
- Death in the Family? Don't Call the Mortician, Call the Taxidermist!
- Tournament Fishing with Your Spouse: Big Mistake or Bad Idea?

IT'S SUMMER. DO YOU KNOW WHERE YOUR HUSBAND IS?

PRINCIPLE #2. Marriage is not a catch-and-release program. It's survival depends on how well you master the Two Essential Marriage Skills: Lying and Arguing.

LYING: Believe me, when a big fishing trip is at stake, deception is the key to matrimonial longevity. When all else fails, lie. Two well-trained liars can maintain a long-lasting relationship that truthful couples can only marvel at with envy. Still not convinced? Let's look at an example of the wrong way to announce an upcoming fishing trip . . . the honest way:

KERN: "Honey, I'd like to go fishing with the guys for the weekend, okay?"
VALERIE: *"Ahhhhhh!* Why do we go over the same thing every week? I think you're trying to drive me crazy! *Ahhhhhhhhhh!"*

    Pathetic. Kern should be headed for the lake. Instead, he's headed straight for Divorce Court. When will he learn to *stop telling the truth and start lying*? Let's see what happens when Kern handles the situation the smart way . . . by lying:

KERN: "Honey, I have bad news. The doctor told me

I have a brain tumor. He's sending me up north to the Gill Fischer Clinic in Lake City. No phone calls, no visitors. I think we'd better go over my life-insurance policy, just in case."

VALERIE: *"Ahhhhh!* Why do we go over the same thing every single week? I think you're trying to drive me crazy! *Ahhhhhhhhhh!"*

See, it works every time! Of course she didn't buy that ridiculous story, but now Kern has a justifiable excuse for marching right out that door with tackle box in hand. After all, he told her he had a *brain tumor*—and she still says no? What an ice cube! He's in the right and he knows it! Now he can leave for a weekend fish fest with an absolutely clear conscience. Whadda guy!

Helpful Hint: Every experienced angler knows, there is a right time and a wrong time to announce your weekend fishing plans. *Never* tell your wife you are going fishing for the weekend when:

- she is defrosting the freezer with an ice pick
- she is experiencing any phase of the PMS cycle
- she has a plate of spaghetti in her hands
- she is watching *Fatal Attraction* or *The Texas Chainsaw Massacre*
- she has the major credit cards in her possession
- she is within reaching distance of your gun collection

ARGUING: When I want to go fishing and my wife gives me that No-way-José look, there is only one thing that will get me out of the house and onto the lake. It works every time. *I start an argument.* Don't get me wrong, I love my wife very much. Sometimes I even act like it. But there are times when I just need to be on the water. And it's during those times that I get desperate. I become the Spatmaster from Hell . . . The Quibble King. With a little practice, you too can learn the time-tested techniques that will enable you, the Spatmaster, to go fishing when all hope for fun seems lost. Quibble Kings are easy to recognize by the ease with which they can spark an argument. Any novice can lock horns over the obvious issues like money, sex, or bait in the fridge. But not the Spatmasters. They will take a seemingly insignificant detail that lesser human beings might overlook

THE EXPERIENCED SPATMASTER IS EASY TO RECOGNIZE BY THE EASE WITH WHICH HE CAN SPARK AN ARGUMENT.

and escalate it into a raging, rip-roaring Oh-my-gawd-I-think-she's-going-to-strangle-him-with-his-own-stringer blowout!

Let's take a look at Maverick, an experienced Spatmaster, and see how he turns what might have been a boring weekend of domestic chores into a fun-filled weekend fish fest:

JILL: "Honey, please blow your nose, it's whistling."
MAV: "You're trying to provoke me, aren't you?"
JILL: "Don't be ridiculous, I only said your nose is whistling. As a matter of fact, it sounds like a teakettle. Blow it, will you please?"
MAV: "What do you mean, my nose looks like a *teakettle?* I can't believe you said that! Especially you, with your mother! Her nose looks like a ripe tomato, and it's no wonder with all the cheap booze she slurps up every night!"

Excellent! Notice how Mav skillfully redirected the focus from his nose to his mother-in-law's drinking problem. He opened up the inlaw floodgates so fast, Jill never knew what hit her. This argument can branch out in any number of directions, giving Maverick plenty of opportunities to storm *out* the door and *into* Fishing Bliss. Way to go, Mav!

Quibble King Tip #1: *Keep it simple.* Don't forget these trivial little irritants. With a little prodding, they can develop into real Squabble Rockets!

♦ nail biting
♦ leaving crumbs on the counter
♦ genital scratching
♦ bathtub hair

Quibble King Tip #2: *Don't forget sarcasm.*
Here are eleven no-fail snappy comebacks to use when you're wrong but won't admit it:

1. It's a free country.
2. La la la . . . I can't hear you . . . la la la.
3. Who the hell died and made you boss?
4. I think you're losing your mind.
5. I know you are, but what am I?
6. You started it.
7. You're trying to provoke me, aren't you?
8. That's so funny I forgot to laugh.
9. I got that from you.
10. Your family warned me about you.
11. Yeah. Sure. Tell me about it.

I KNOW YOU ARE, BUT WHAT AM I ?

REMEMBER THE RULES:
NO SPITTING, NO HITTING...

Quibble King Tip #3: *Strive for maximum flare-up.*

- For maximum flare-up, begin each accusation with *"you always"* or *"you never."* This is guaranteed to inflame any issue, no matter how trivial, into a major, full-blown door-slammer.
- Gain extra mileage from those old worn-out issues by leaving each disagreement unresolved. Remember; unresolved conflicts are ticking bombs, just waiting to explode again and again.
- Remember the rules: no spitting, no hitting.

PRINCIPLE #3: *Marriage, Change, and the Irritant Factor will suck your brain dry.* Marriage has a way of changing things, and let's face it, nobody likes change. In fact, you'll find the word "change" at the top of everybody's "Things I Would Like to Burn in Hell" list. Personally, I give it an Irritant Factor rating of Plus 10. That's even higher than I rate some of the Irritant Classics like dull hooks, snags, or the absolute worst—sheephead feeding frenzies.

Every angler will tell you, the first thing to change after you're married will be your relationship with your fishing buddies. Most of us have old work pals or ex-cellmates with whom we shared many important experiences, like drinking and throwing up on each other. Or fishing all night. Once you get married, all that will have to change. A typical before-and-after conversation between fishing buddies might go something like this:

Single Buddies: "Hey, let's stay and fish the night bite!"
Single You: *"Yesss! Totally awesome! Let's do it!"*
Married You: "I don't know, guys. This will be the fifth night in a row. It just wouldn't be fair to Mary.

Well ... okay, but just twelve more hours, then I really have to go!"

If all this is causing your brain to feel like a Veg-O-Matic set on Max, don't sweat it. That's normal. You'll do just fine if you remember one thing: In any successful marriage, it is vital that each partner understand the wants and needs of the opposite sex. Generally speaking, they go pretty much like this:

A WOMAN'S WANTS AND NEEDS:
romance, intimacy, back rubs, affection, and occasional hugs.

A MAN'S WANTS AND NEEDS:
cheap bait and plenty of it.

Excessive fishing can cause unmanageable problems in our lives. For example, you know it's time to re-evaluate your priorities when you catch yourself sizing up all-night 7-Eleven stores because the high cost of bait and tackle has strained your budget to the max. There are other warning signs you should watch out for. Take the following quiz to see if you are approaching the Danger Zone.

Fishermen on the Faultline Quiz

(Circle the answer that most applies to you.)

1. **You return home from a week-long fishing trip. Your wife:**
   a. welcomes you with hugs and kisses and presents you with a new monogrammed fishing vest
   b. politely introduces you to her new husband
   c. reaches for the AK-47 and hollow-point bullets

2. **You return home from an extra-long fishing trip. Your children:**
   a. squeal with delight and show you the fishing drawings they made while you were away
   b. stare vacantly at the TV and don't acknowledge you
   c. are in jail awaiting bail

3. **You return home from an extra-, extra-long fishing trip. Upon your arrival, you find:**
   a. a six-foot banner stretched across your porch that says, "Welcome home to the best fishing dad in the world!"

b. your entire tackle and trophy collection for sale on the front lawn

c. the pizza delivery boy lounging in your bathrobe and drinking your beer

4. **Your family sends you to the video store. You return with:**
   a. *Bambi, E.T.*
   b. *Moby Dick, The Old Man and the Sea.*
   c. Instructional fishing videos, including *Spoon Pluggin' with Buck, Stink-Bait Preparation*, and *Big Muskies Love Live Rats.*

5. **Your wife's obstetrician has just informed you she is due to deliver the same weekend as the big fishing tournament. Overwhelmed with disbelief, you:**
   a. drop out of the tournament and sign up for extra birth classes
   b. convert the live well into a baby crib
   c. every chance you get, you sneak up behind her and scream bloody murder, hoping to induce an early delivery

100

6. Your family complains that you have been fishing too much and ignoring them. After serious contemplation, you decide to:
   a. fish less and spend more *quality* time with them
   b. announce a big family fishing vacation up north
   c. cock your head to one side, howl out *"Bad Seeeeeeed,"* and reach for the chainsaw.

7. Your children's school has scheduled their annual bazaar for the same weekend as the fishing opener. You think it over and decide to:
   a. thoughtfully cancel your fishing plans and volunteer to help
   b. pull the kids from school and bus them to the next district
   c. torch the friggin' school.

KEY

If you answered "a" to five or more questions, congratulations! You have achieved a healthy balance between fishing and marriage.

If you answered "b" to five or more questions, your situation is about normal, which means you are going to have to find a new excuse for your excessive drinking.

If you answered "c" to five or more questions, the situation is hopeless. Do what I do. Try not to think about it and go fishing instead.

I WONDER WHAT IT MEANS IF YOU ANSWER "C" TO EVERYTHING?

"JEFFREY, I **REALLY** THINK YOU SHOULD SEE A DOCTOR."

"WHAT'S THERE TO DISCUSS?"

MIKE HAS A MOMENTARY LAPSE OF REASONING...

"I'M AFRAID ROBERT HAS A TERMINAL CASE OF... BOBBERS."

"IT JUST WOULDN'T BE HAROLD WITHOUT HIS FISHING VEST AND ROD."

"MY GOD, HARRY, PROMISE ME
YOU'LL NEVER GO SALTWATER FISHING AGAIN!"

"DAD SAYS THE FOUR MAJOR FOOD GROUPS
ARE MINNOWS, NIGHTCRAWLERS, LEECHES AND CRABS."

RALPH TOLD HIS FAMILY ABOUT HIS SECRET AMBITION:
TO BECOME A PROFESSIONAL FISHERMAN.

Catalog Pages from Tackle Heaven

Tackle catalogs are, without question, my favorite form of literature. Browsing through the ol' Bliss Book keeps my mind off life's nagging little problems. Like the fact that my tackle collection has grown so large, my wife has threatened to open it to the public and charge admission. I know she is serious because large sweaty workers have been hammering away on our front lawn for days, erecting a giant sign that says:

VISIT **THE TACKLE KINGDOM**, THE MOST EXCESSIVE TACKLE COLLECTION IN THE HISTORY OF THE WORLD! WITNESS THE INCREDIBLE *3-OF-EVERY-SIZE-IN-EVERY-COLOR* CHAMBER, MARVEL AT THE UNFORGETTABLE HALL OF HOOKS! INCREDIBLE AS IT MAY SEEM, VIRTUALLY NONE OF IT PAID FOR!

I would hate to have strange people walking through my tackle room, actually *touching my things.*

Then again, it could be worse. The workers could be erecting the sign I caught my wife secretly sketching out the other day:

MAJOR TACKLE CLEARANCE SALE
DUE TO VIOLENT DEATH OF HUSBAND.
EVERYTHING MUST GO!

Spooky. But true.

Four out of five Angling Addicts agree: the marketing copy you read in Binge Books is so totally absurd, you'd think the typical tackle writer is a lobotomy recipient who lacks a working brain. Try to imagine him, if you can, drooling down his Hawaiian shirt while awkwardly scrawling out lure copy using a blunt crayon on oversized sheets of paper. Every now and then, his lone brain cell sputters and pops, then reluctantly kicks in just long enough to scrawl out one more bizarre glob of marketing mumbo-jumbo:

115

it's Hawg Calling action is your one way ticket to PIG CITY!!

Don't get me wrong, I *like* reading tackle catalogs. In fact, what cracks me up the most are those really off-the-wall lure names. You know the ones I'm talking about. You read them and think *phew*—totally out to lunch! I'd like to shake the hand of the genius who makes up those names, but such a person probably doesn't exist. The names just kind of *appear*, like magic, from the outer regions of the Tackle Twilight Zone.

I like to play a game where I rate the really bizarre names, then I take the winners and induct them into:

The Lure Name Hall of Shame

The Ripple Pig®—with activated Pig Juice® inside!

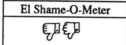

Am I crazy, or does this sound more like a wino with a hygiene problem than it does a lure name?

Dumpster Juice® fish scent—Formulated to attract only the meanest Junkyard Hawgs!

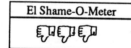

I'm speechless. I'm also tempted.

Lil' Squirmie Squirt® crappie jigs—Collect 'em, trade 'em! The Squirm family includes: Lil' Fuzz-E-Squirt, Lil' Furr-E-Squirt and Lil' Bitty Squirt.

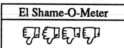

Awww, poor Squirmie gets 4 Lil' Thumbies down, too bad. Notice those clever misspellings.

That alone makes me want to run right out and buy a hundred of them. I'm surprised they didn't dot the i's with happy faces or daisies.

The Slimy Shad®—featuring Real Fish Slime!

El Shame-O-Meter
👎👎👎👎👎👎

Excuse me while I blow chunks! This name rocked the El Shame-O-Meter, not to mention the Vomit Meter! This is definitely not something I would want in my tackle box. It sounds more like something I would bury out behind the garage.

I don't know about you, but the way I figure it, there must be three basic laws that all tackle companies follow when they develop lures. Because without exception, every lure I own has all of the following characteristics:

The Three Basic Laws of Lure Making

LAW #1: THE BLUNT-TIP LAW. All lures *must* have dull hooks. This has to be a law. How else would you explain the fact that 98 percent of the lures I buy have hooks so dull, they could be used as day-care-center toys?

LAW #2: THE SNAG MAGNET LAW. This is similar to the Light Bulb Law. You know, they burn out after one hundred hours when they could be made to last ten times that long. Well, crank baits are manufactured in a similar way—only, they are absolutely, positively guaranteed to snag within fifteen casts. For jigs, the number drops to three casts.

LET ME SEE... I'LL BE FISHING FOR ABOUT 5 HOURS. THAT MEANS I'LL PROBABLY NEED ABOUT 8,746 JIGS.

LAW #3: THE FAMOUS PERSONALITY LAW. In order to be successful in the catalog business, a lure must be endorsed by no less than fifty Famous Pro Anglers that no one has ever heard of.

I once saw a fishing show where some famous guy I never heard of tied on a buzz bait and proceeded to catch about ten thousand bass in less than thirty minutes. Minus commercials. So naturally, I am now *heavily* into buzz baits. I even bought one of those blue oval name patches for my fishing shirt. You know, the kind all the gas station guys wear? It has the name *Buzz* embroidered on it, and I think that's cool. I guess that proves I'm a sucker for hype. It also indicates that I may be just as addicted to tackle as I am to fishing. How about you?

- Does your IN CASE OF EMERGENCY telephone list have a tackle catalog 800 number on it? Is the 800 number listed ahead of the police and fire department? Oh-oh . . .
- When you get bored at work, do you find yourself inventing lure prototypes using paperclips and other office supplies? Hmmmm?
- How about this one: have you ever given your lure a little pep talk before casting it out? Tsk, tsk, tsk.

Sound familiar? If it does, I recommend you take the following test to find out if you are in fact . . . Addicted to Tackle:

The Addicted-to-Tackle Test

Circle the answer that best describes the way you would react:

1. **When you drive by your favorite tackle store, you usually:**
   a. look to see who's working
   b. run in for a few small items
   c. salivate profusely

2. **You're tackle shopping and some busybody tells you that your tackle selection is all wrong. You consider his comment and:**
   a. politely ignore him
   b. politely introduce him to your middle finger
   c. politely introduce his face to the jig bin

3. **You consider tackle catalogs to be:**
   a. a convenient form of shopping
   b. a vital form of American literature
   c. the primary reason you declared bankruptcy

4. You're in the middle of the Big Tournament. Suddenly, you lose your last lure to a snag. You quickly weigh your options and decide to:
   a. call it a day
   b. improvise and make do with what little tackle you have
   c. clench your fillet knife between your teeth and raise the Skull and Crossbones

5. Your catalog order is slow to arrive by mail. The mailman shows up *again* without your tackle. You gather your thoughts and:
   a. express your concern to him
   b. express your extreme displeasure to the main office
   c. Federal Express his remains to the complaint department

6. You receive your monthly statement from Visa. You:
   a. are mildly surprised by the amount of tackle you charged
   b. suffer a wave of guilt because of the high tackle charges
   c. suffer a massive coronary

7. In order to pay the increasing costs of tackle, you have considered:
   a. making do with what you have
   b. setting up shop in the basement and making your own tackle
   c. setting up shop in the basement and making your own money

8. You realize that your new fishing partner is actually a lure leech. You can't believe your ears when, for the fifth time, he says, "Lend me a couple more jigs, will ya, buddy?" Amazed, you:
   a. give him the jigs
   b. give him the jigs, plus a menacing glare
   c. give him A Whole New Outlook on Life

9. The sound of the mailman closing your mailbox lid reminds you of:
   a. your recent tackle order
   b. your past-due Visa bill
   c. Pavlov's Door

10. You're in the Mega Tackle Store when suddenly you realize you're out of control and have been compulsively stuffing tackle

into your cart for over an hour.
Unable to pay, you decide to:

a. return each item to its proper rack
b. ditch the cart
c. grab a ski mask and make
one last selection . . . at
the gun counter

KEY

If you answered "a" to six or more questions, relax, you're fine. You're probably the type of person who can walk out of a tackle store empty-handed. I have heard that people like you exist, it's just that I never met anyone who would admit to it.

If you answered "b" to six or more questions, not to worry: when it comes to tackle, you're normal. You're just a little boring.

However, if you answered "c" to six or more questions: Sorry. At least now you understand the rubbery legs and trembling hands every time you open a tackle catalog. Cheer up, the situation isn't terminal, in fact there are treatment options available to you: There's always the local funny farm. I understand they offer a pretty good selection of basket-weaving courses. Or if you're into *sharing*, you might want to try a support group. On the other hand, you could do what we Heavy Hitters do: Invent-O-Therapy. That's where you invent the type of tackle you would like to see in your favorite catalog. It works wonders! I've included some of my favorite items on the following pages. Check it out!

CATALOG ITEMS I'D LIKE TO SEE...

FIB-SLING® EMERGENCY EXCUSE BANDAGES

Late again because the fish were/weren't biting? Need a good excuse? This baby not only gets you out of a tight spot, it will actually arouse sympathy and understanding in even the most skeptical spouse. The FIB-SLING® is 100% cotton and comes pre-stained and soiled to simulate a realistic injury wrap. Blood pump included. Artificial broken limbs available featuring our patented E-Z Hide™ harness system.
ORDER: O-MAGAWD!

CAP SNUG

This handy little item eliminates unsightly cap turn-around during high-speed boat travel. Now you can make a bassin' fashion statement while zooming from hot spot to honey hole. Stress due to cap fly-off is a thing of the past, and our sporty vinyl straps blend nicely with face and head. Also available in reflective white for use during night fishing. Pro-Snug model—exactly the same as above only $5 more expensive. ORDER: B'LONY

CATALOG ITEMS I'D LIKE TO SEE...

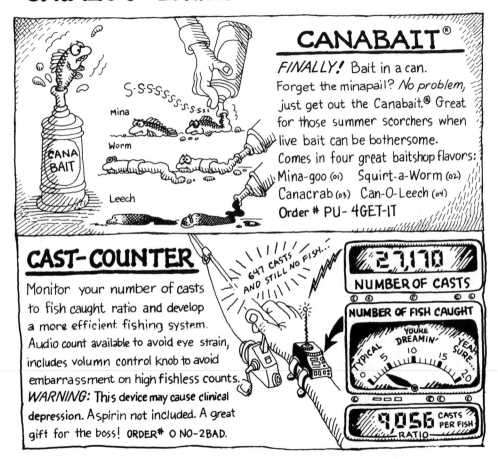

CANABAIT®

FINALLY! Bait in a can. Forget the minapail? *No problem,* just get out the Canabait.® Great for those summer scorchers when live bait can be bothersome. Comes in four great baitshop flavors:

Mina-goo (01)   Squirt-a-Worm (02)
Canacrab (03)   Can-O-Leech (04)

Order # PU-4GET-IT

CAST-COUNTER

Monitor your number of casts to fish caught ratio and develop a more efficient fishing system. Audio count available to avoid eye strain, includes volumn control knob to avoid embarrassment on high fishless counts. *WARNING:* This device may cause clinical depression. Aspirin not included. A great gift for the boss! ORDER# O NO-2BAD.

CATALOG ITEMS I'D LIKE TO SEE...

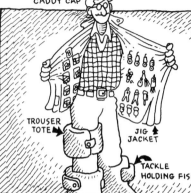

CADDY CAP

TROUSER TOTE

JIG JACKET

TACKLE HOLDING FISHING BOOTS

BASSIN' FASHION™

Our newest line of sporty leisure garments were developed for the New Age Fishermen that demand fashion *and* function from their tackle and leisure wearage. Each garment features modern styling with E-Z Hide® tackle storage units. All Bassin' Fashion™ garments feature our patented **FINSULATE**® single layer construction.

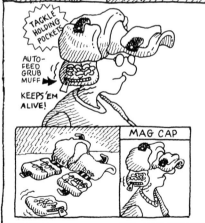

TACKLE HOLDING POCKETS

AUTO-FEED GRUB MUFF

KEEPS 'EM ALIVE!

MAG CAP

CADDY CAP®

Here's a smart little number that's equally at home in the bass buggy or at the office. This alluring cap features three Flex-O-Pockets® that transform your unsightly collection of loose lures into a well organized *tackle management system*. Large capacity storage units are constructed of rugged wormproof materials. Velcro closures are designed for quick, efficient and noiseless lure selection. Optional features include detachable auto-feed Grub Muff and clip on Pig Pocket.
ORDER: O·NO!

CATALOG ITEMS I'D LIKE TO SEE...

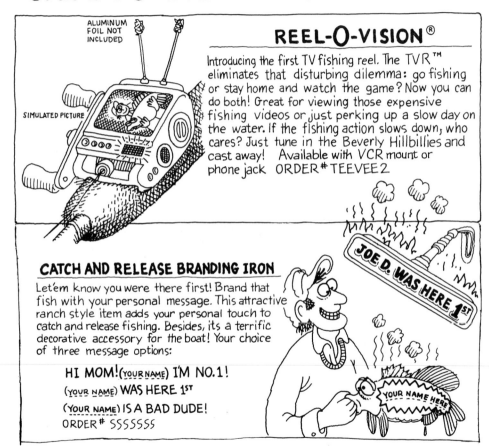

ALUMINUM FOIL NOT INCLUDED

SIMULATED PICTURE

REEL-O-VISION ®

Introducing the first TV fishing reel. The TVR™ eliminates that disturbing dilemma: go fishing or stay home and watch the game? Now you can do both! Great for viewing those expensive fishing videos or just perking up a slow day on the water. If the fishing action slows down, who cares? Just tune in the Beverly Hillbillies and cast away! Available with VCR mount or phone jack ORDER # TEEVEE 2

CATCH AND RELEASE BRANDING IRON

Let'em know you were there first! Brand that fish with your personal message. This attractive ranch style item adds your personal touch to catch and release fishing. Besides, it's a terrific decorative accessory for the boat! Your choice of three message options:

HI MOM! (YOUR NAME) I'M NO.1!

(YOUR NAME) WAS HERE 1ST

(YOUR NAME) IS A BAD DUDE!

ORDER # SSSSSS

JOE D. WAS HERE 1ST

YOUR NAME HERE

CATALOG ITEMS I'D LIKE TO SEE...

KEEPS'EM COOL!

THE BAIT BLASTER™

Our revolutionary bucket design features a built in AM/FM cassette player. This *boom bucket* minimizes accessory clutter and utilizes available boat space in an efficient and stylish manner. *Sluggish bait?* No problem—*just crank it up!* Vibrations resulting from heavy metal power chords invigorate even the most lethargic minas. The Bait Blaster® features our patented Sure-Seal® lid and No Hassle® bait retrieval system. Specify Designer Blaster(oı) or Shoulder Blaster(o₂). Rugged enamel finish options: Ghetto Graffiti (A) Tiger Stripe (B) Reggae Motif (C). ORDER: BAITAMAX

THE BASSIN' BUDDIE™

Finally! Fish-finding technology with the human touch. The PBB® (PERSONAL BASSIN' BUDDIE) is an attractively styled fish locating unit that features a stunningly realistic head mount which *actually verbalizes incoming data.* The well modulated electronic voice *softy verbalizes* a variety of information including depth range, bottom content, trolling speed, beer cooler temperature and tonights cable listings. The *Variable Voice Control* allows you to program a loudness range from a whisper up to the screaming fish alarm. Rotary eyes light up for night usage.
ORDER: LO-TEC

...BIG BASS OFF THE WEEDLINE AT TEN FEET, HAL...

INCREDIBLY REALISTIC!

Please, practice Selective Harvesting: Keep the little guys for the frying pan and release the big spawners to replenish God's precious resource.

And if you can, take a kid fishing. I'm forever grateful someone took me.

GEORGE PETERS